LIGHTNING BOLT BOOKS™

Boxers

Sarah Frank

Lerner Publications ◆ Minneapolis

Lerner Publications Company
A division of Lerner Publishing Group, Inc.
241 First Avenue North
Minneapolis, MN 55401 USA

For reading levels and more information, look up this title at www.lernerbooks.com.

Library of Congress Cataloging-in-Publication Data

Names: Frank, Sarah, author.
Title: Boxers / Sarah Frank.
Description: Minneapolis : Lerner Publications, [2019] | Series: Lightning Bolt Books. Who's a good dog? | Audience: Age 6-9. | Audience: Grade K to 3. | Includes bibliographical references and index.
Identifiers: LCCN 2018034350 (print) | LCCN 2018035823 (ebook) | ISBN 9781541556614 (eb pdf) | ISBN 9781541555716 (lb : alk. paper)
Subjects: LCSH: Boxer (Dog breed)—Juvenile literature.
Classification: LCC SF429.B75 (ebook) | LCC SF429.B75 F73 2019 (print) | DDC 636.73—dc23

LC record available at https://lccn.loc.gov/2018034350

Manufactured in the United States of America
1 - 46026 - 43349 - 10/29/2018

Table of Contents

A Playful Pooch

You walk in the door. Your boxer runs to greet you with a kiss. Boxers are the best!

Boxers often race to greet their owners.

Boxers are active and fun loving. These dogs weigh about 65 to 80 pounds (29 to 36 kg). You can't miss a happy boxer heading your way!

Boxers are usually fawn or brindle. Fawn boxers may be tan to deep reddish brown. Brindle dogs are brown with black stripes.

Some boxers have white markings, and others are all white.

All boxers are fun to be around. They are playful and sweet. And their owners just love them!

Boxer History

At first, all boxers worked. They herded animals and guarded homes. The American Kennel Club (AKC) groups dogs by what they do or how they act. It puts boxers in the working group.

Some boxers still work. They might work as therapy dogs. Therapy dogs visit people on bed rest or in hospitals. They help patients feel better.

Petting therapy dogs helps patients feel better.

Working dogs come from different parts of the world. Boxers come from Germany.

The standard schnauzer is another working dog from *Germany*.

In the 1930s, boxers became
popular in the United States.
They are still popular today.
Many families have
boxers as pets.

The Dog for You?

Would you like a boxer puppy? Boxers need a special kind of owner. Talk with your family to decide if a boxer is for you.

Boxers have tons of energy. A boxer might have fun running in circles around your home. Would this bother your family? If so, pass on a boxer.

Bored boxers can get into trouble.

Boxers are smart. They need people and toys to play with. If you're gone a lot, don't get a boxer.

Do you want a pooch that follows you everywhere? A boxer may do this. If you're a loner, think about getting a cat.

Welcome, Boxer!

Does your family still want a boxer? Then it's time to buy supplies. Boxers need food, bowls, toys, and more.

Your family also needs to find your boxer a vet. The vet will examine your boxer.

Vets take good care of dogs.

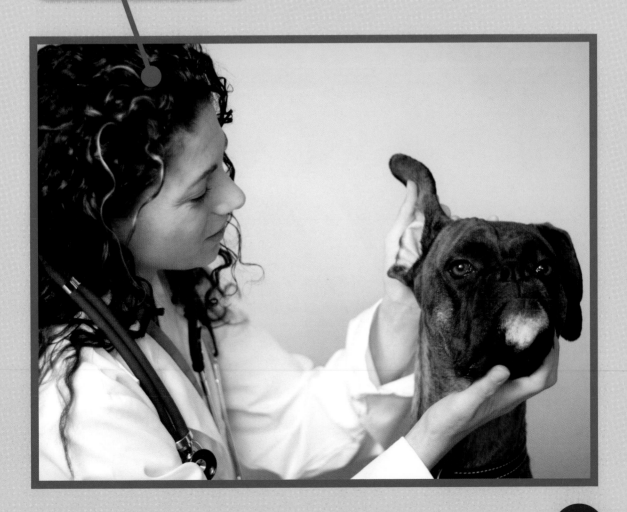

You'll need to groom your boxer. Boxers sometimes shed. Brushing will cut down on this.

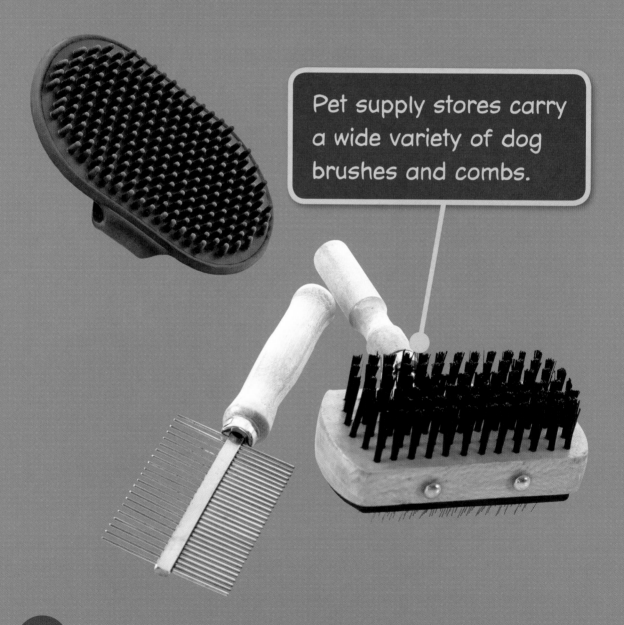

Pet supply stores carry a wide variety of dog brushes and combs.

You and your boxer are in for lots of fun. Take good care of your new pet. Be the kind of owner your boxer can be proud of.

Doggone Good Tips!

- Looking for a great name for your boxer? Here are some ideas: Chance, Iris, Willow, Disco, Buckaroo, Jasper, or Jessica.

- White boxers are more likely to be deaf in one or both ears. So they may rely on their senses of smell and sight even more than most other boxers.

- Make sure you have plenty of space in your home and yard if you get a boxer. Boxers need room to play and run around!

Why Boxers Are the Best

- Boxers helped the German army during World War I (1914–1918). They carried messages and did other jobs for soldiers.

- Some boxers act as search and rescue dogs. These heroic pooches find people after disasters.

- Boxers often jump up and raise their front paws. It's supercute—and it makes them look a little like human boxers! That may be where their name comes from.

Glossary

American Kennel Club (AKC): an organization that groups dogs by breed

bed rest: the need to stay in bed due to serious illness

brindle: brown with black stripes

fawn: a shade of brown

groom: to brush and clean a dog's coat

herd: to make animals move together as a group

therapy dog: a dog that visits people who are ill or in nursing homes

vet: a doctor who treats animals

working group: a group of dogs bred to do different kinds of jobs

Further Reading

American Kennel Club
https://www.akc.org

American Society for the Prevention of Cruelty to
Animals
https://www.aspca.org

Fishman, Jon M. *Hero Therapy Dogs*. Minneapolis:
Lerner Publications, 2017.

Hansen, Grace. *Boxers*. Minneapolis: Abdo Kids, 2017.

Rustad, Martha E. H. *Boxers*. Mankato, MN Amicus
High Interest, 2018.

Index

Photo Acknowledgments

Image credits: otsphoto/Shutterstock.com, p. 2; tshortell/Getty Images, p. 4; Lisjatina/ Shutterstock.com, p. 5; atikinka/Shutterstock.com, p. 6; Jupiterimages/Getty Images, p. 7; Vera Zinkova/Shutterstock.com, p. 8; Anna Hoychuk/Shutterstock.com, p. 9; Jne Valokuvaus/Shutterstock.com, p. 10; Hurst Photo/Shutterstock.com, p. 11; fotojagodka/ Getty Images, p. 12; everydoghasastory/Shutterstock.com, p. 13; Jacobs Stock Photography/Getty Images, p. 14; Julia Pleskachevskaia/Shutterstock.com, p. 15; Niklas Heisters/Shutterstock.com, p. 16; lumenphoto/Getty Images, p. 17; Birgit Reitz-Hofmann/ Shutterstock.com, p. 18; Diyosa Carter/Getty Images, p. 19; Gerald Marella/Shutterstock. com, p. 23.

Cover: MarkCoffeyPhoto/Getty Images.

Main body text set in Billy Infant regular 28/36. Typeface provided by SparkType.